D1681424

STECK-VAUGHN
NEW WAY
HEADS and TAILS

Zoom!

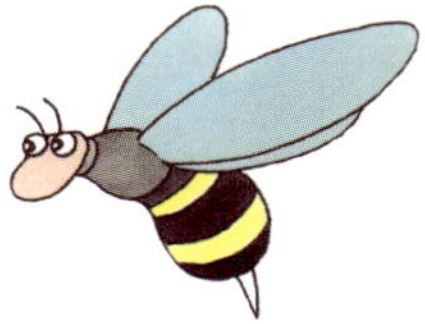

STECK-VAUGHN
COMPANY

A Division of Harcourt Brace & Company

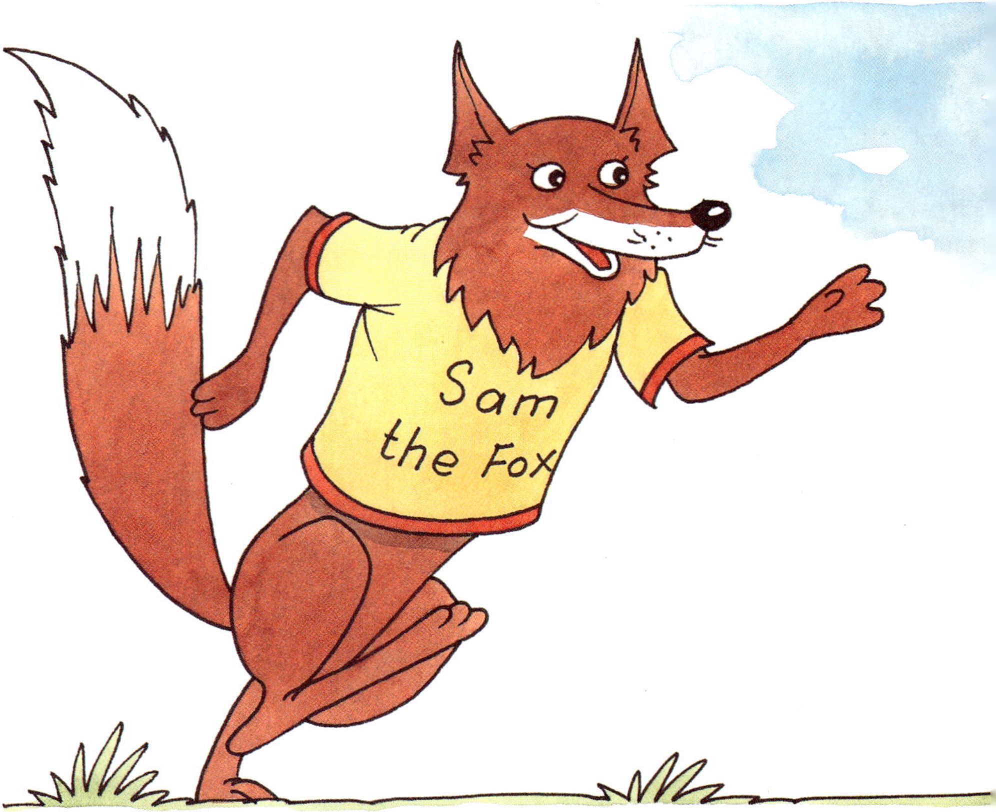

Sam the fox

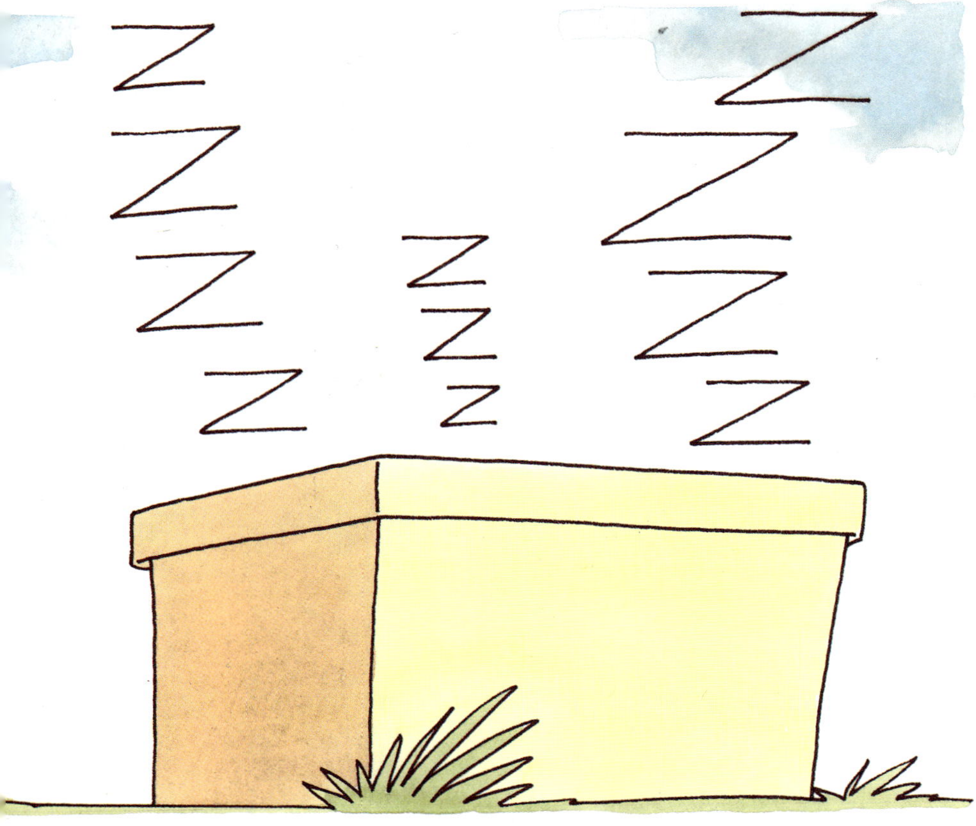

a buzzing box

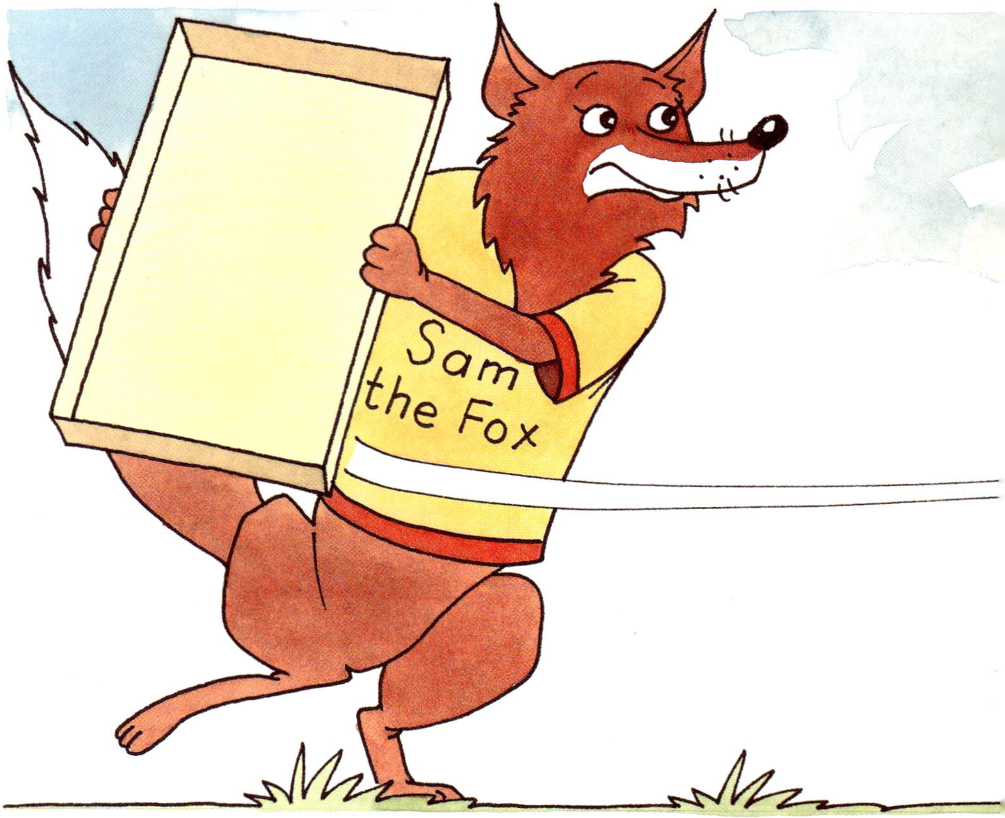

an open box

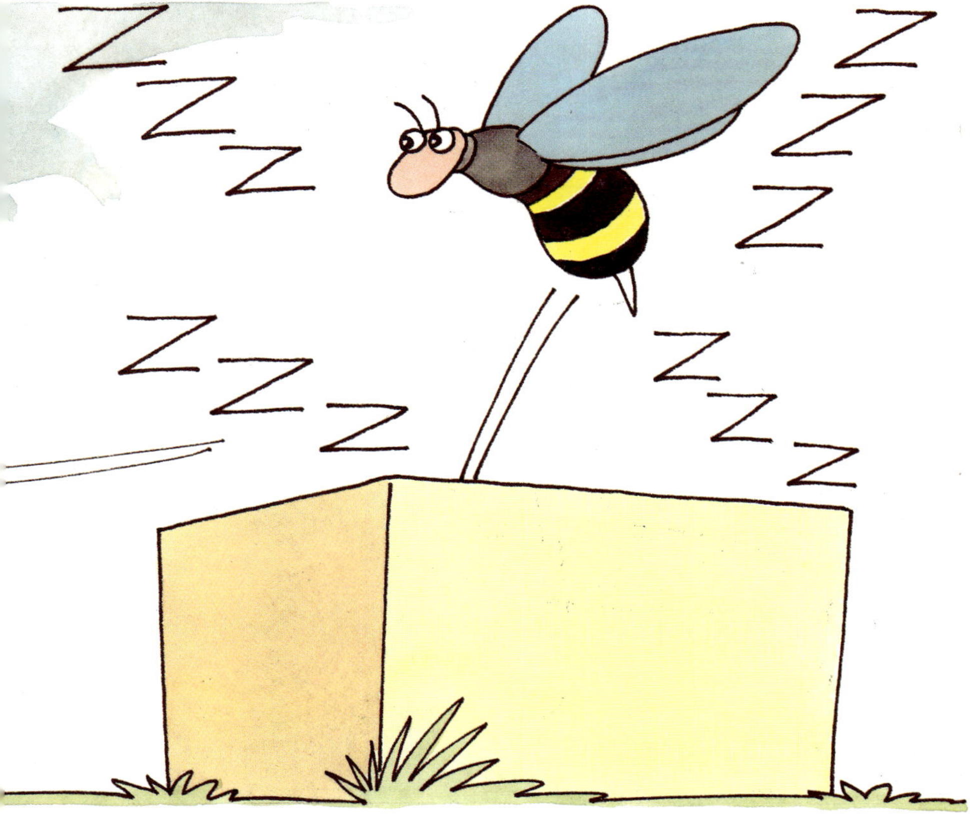

a buzzing bee

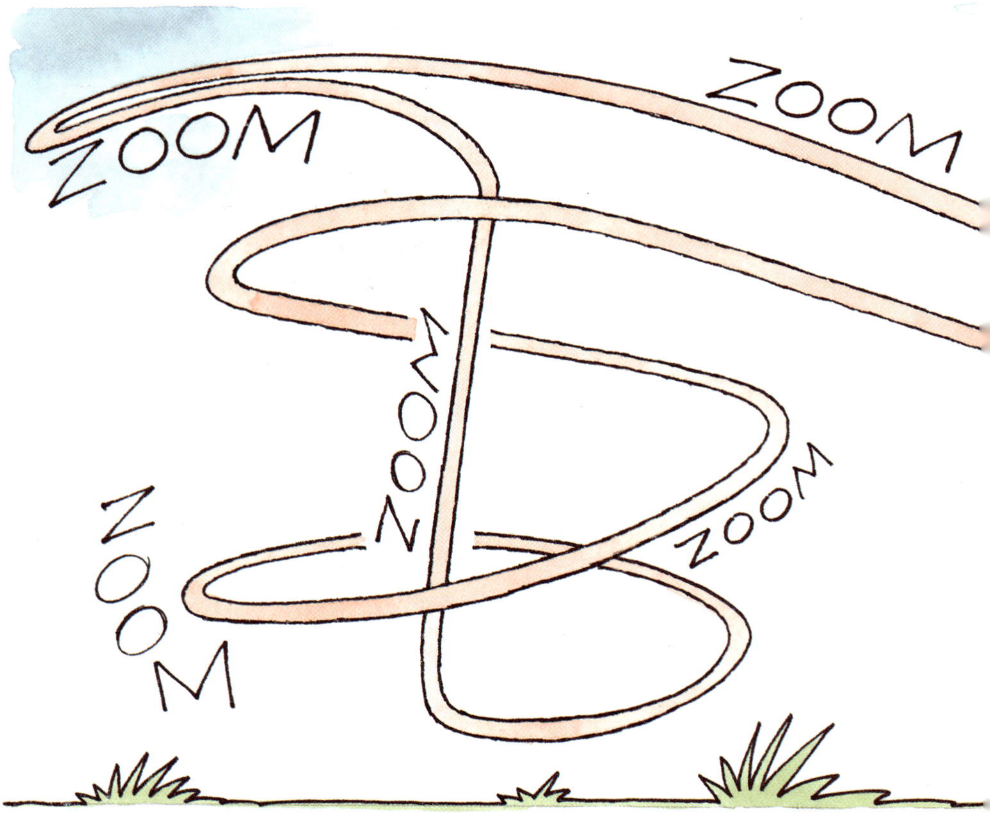

Zoom!

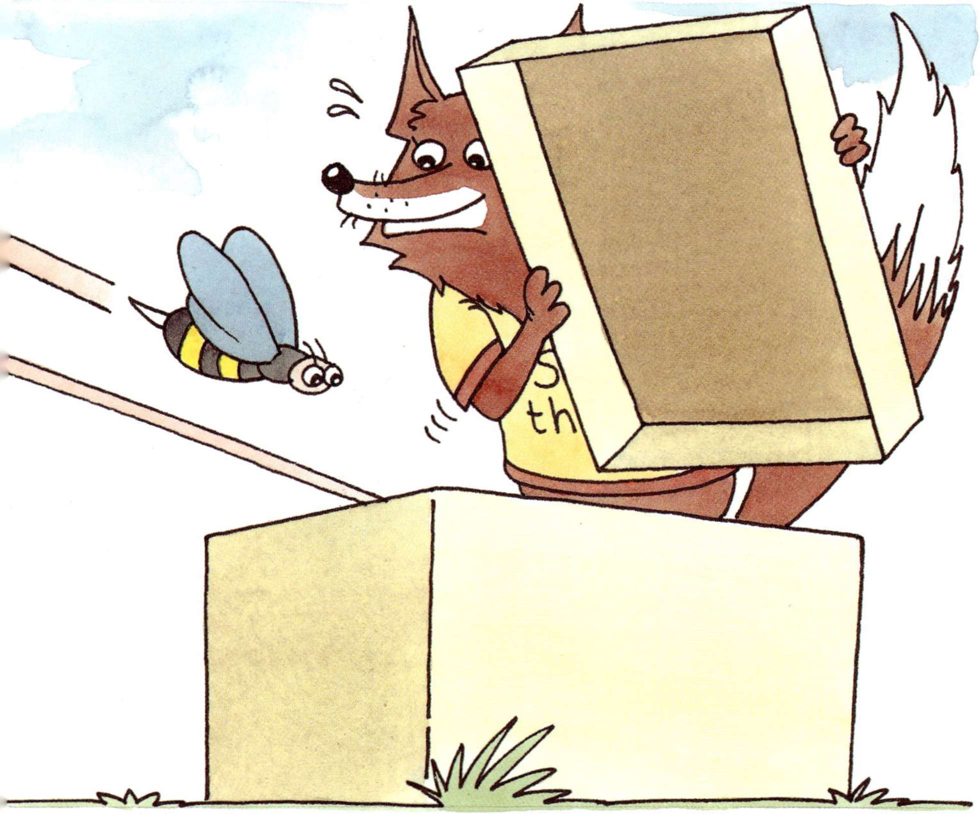

back in the box

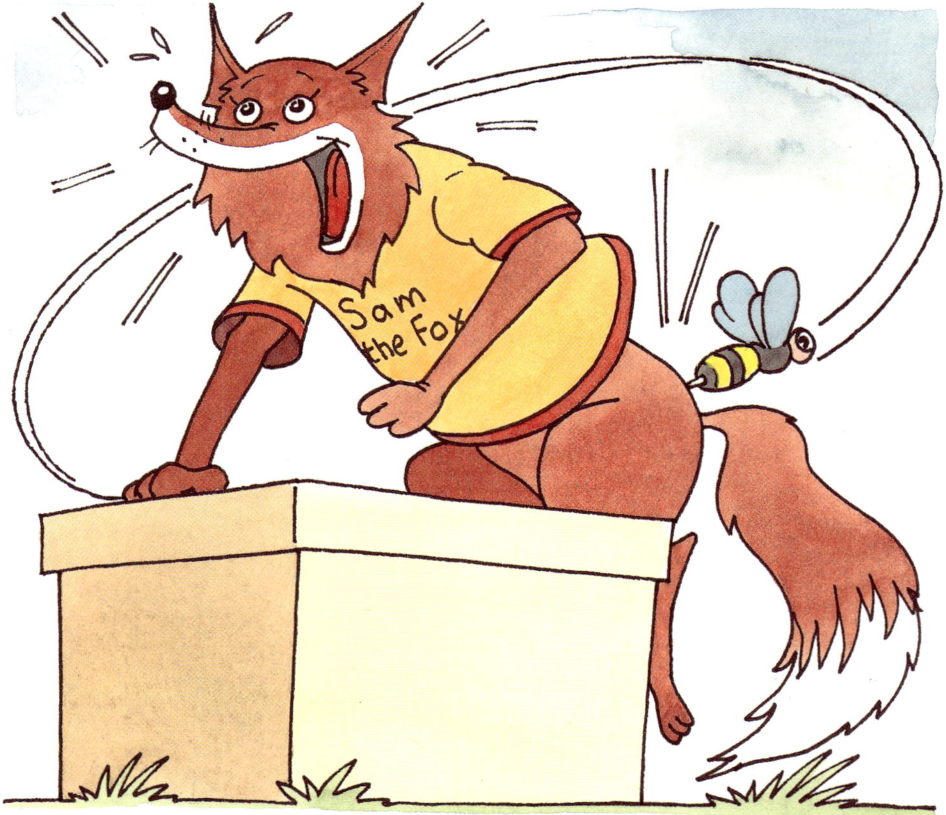

Zap!